DOG FOOD & TREAT RECIPES

With feeding guide by Bev Cobley

Jamie Shanks

Bishopton Dog Walking Services

Contents

How To Feed Your Dog

By Bev Cobley

A suitable diet encompasses all of the essential and non-essential amino acids, balanced with carbohydrates, fats, vitamins, minerals and water; thus providing the dog with a healthy intake of all the necessary nutrients. Although it is important that the diet is palatable to the dog it is important that it is easily digestible and adequate to meet the individual needs of the dog according to age, health and activities. Dog nutrition should be a concern to all dog managers/carers because 'optimal nutrition underlies optimal health' Barbara Fougere, BSCBVMS (hons).

An Appropriate Diet

A species-appropriate diet, sometimes called 'barf' or 'natural' – is based on raw protein intake from uncooked meaty bones, vegetables and fruit; cooked/pulped only when necessary to break down cellulose in order to aid digestion, limited gluten-rich grain, rice and 2nd class protein in the form of cheese, nuts etc. or home cooked. The ancestors of today's dogs would naturally have consumed the whole body of their prey; bones, flesh, organs, gut contents; for fibre, skin and feathers, all of which provided the correct balance of nutrients to sustain them. In today's society this is no longer an option for most of us and meaty bones are not an adequate substitution of a whole carcass, but by adding raw meat, vegetables, fruit, seed and suitable grain, we can offer a close equivalent of this form of a natural diet. This type of diet, if monitored and adjusted accordingly, will provide all the nutrients a dog needs for a healthy, active life. It will ensure good levels of energy, easy digestion, healthy skin and coat, maintain teeth and gums, in fact all the things that commercial food manufacturers promise. This type of diet is more cost-effective than a commercial diet but it is more time consuming and does require management.

Commercial Diets

Commercial diets, whilst easy to use, requiring little or no management, are costly and poorly protected by legislation. Manufacturers are constantly on the lookout for cheap ingredients and will alter recipes accordingly; this is the foremost reason why the wording on their packaging material is so vague; as these changes can be made to the contents without the expenses of reprinting. Commercial foods generally have a higher level of poor quality protein and chemically flavoured fats, these ingredients being more palatable to the dog, with colourings added in order for the food to look more palatable to humans. The title of such foods can be misleading and the use of words like 'premium', 'whole health' and 'meaty goodness' is intended to install confidence.

Converting Dry Matter Basis

This can be the hard part. All pet foods have different levels of moisture. Canned foods can have up to 80% moisture whereas; some dry foods can have as little as 6%. This is important for 2 reasons. The first is that the food is priced by the pound, and when you buy dog food that is 80% water you get 20% food and the rest is water. So the amount of food your pet consumes is small and expensive. The other reason for understanding percent moisture is to help you compare crude protein and fat between brands and between canned and dry. The listings on the label are for the food as it is, not as it would be on a dry matter basis. So without converting both brands of food to a dry matter basis you will not be able to compare them accurately.

If a dry dog food has 10% moisture we know that it has 90% dry matter. So we look at the label and check the protein level that reads 20%. Next, we divide the 20 percent protein by the 90% dry matter and we get 22%, which is the amount of protein on a dry matter basis. Does this make sense so far? Good. Now let us compare this to canned food that has 80% moisture. We know that with 80% moisture we have 20% dry matter. The label shows

5% protein. So we take the 5% and divide it by 20% and we get 25% protein on a dry matter basis. So the canned food has more protein per pound on a dry matter basis after all the water is taken out.

If we take a well known brand of complete food for example; which is quite expensive, the packaging reads 'lamb and rice – gluten free', upon reading the label there is only 4% lamb, 2% meaty extract (whatever that is) and 5% brown rice, the remainder seemed to be made up of soluble fats, soya, beet pulp (left over sugar beet from sugar manufacturers), syrup and yeast. Plus all the 'extra vitamin and minerals, some of which exceeded the r.d.a. and some which don't, assuming there is an even mix between bag and bowl. In the analysis it states 24% protein – well if the meat content is only 4% what is the source of the rest? The big bonus is the 'extract of Yucca – widely acclaimed for its flatulence and fecal odour reducing properties' well that's ok then – no smelly dogs!!

Most carers who feed their dogs on commercial food rely on the so called expertise of the manufacturers, who in reality take advantage of the complicated science of nutrition by limiting factual information whilst at the same time exposing a gullible public to marketing material designed to provide reassurance that the dogs' needs are being catered for.

A good example of this is the following quote taken from the advertising literature for a major brand. 'Very few pet foods are processed and cooked as thoroughly, as slowly and as 'hot' as the xxxxx line of dog foods. You can see how processing every bit as important as the ingredients is. You can also see why a label only tells part of the story'. Well, I don't know about you but actually I would like the label to tell the whole story.

A few years ago we rescued a clumber spaniel called Zak, a 4-year-old male, with a very bad ulcerating skin condition, which also affected his larynx and colon. Since leaving the breeder he had only been fed on the same, popular, dry complete food; on the basis that 'anything else makes him really poorly and upsets his stomach' he was allowed 'half an apple or carrot once per day',

his carers genuinely believed that his skin and ulcerated internal tissue to be a genetic condition. They had spent a fortune on prescriptions and tests and as the condition started when he was still a very young puppy, the insurance companies would not cover the treatment cost. The food he was on was sold through the veterinary practice that had been treating him and was in fact recommended by their veterinary surgeon as a suitable diet. Tearfully leaving him, with strict instruction not to change his diet, along with 3 months supply of 2 types of antibiotic; one broad spectrum for 'better days' and one specific for 'bad days', 3 months supply of steroids and a homeopathic tea tree lotion, we didn't know whether to weep for the dog or the people. It took us 3 months to gradually change his diet and reduce his antibiotic and steroidal intake. We increased his food to 70% home produced/raw and boosted his immune system with the extra minerals and vitamins, C, B2, Biotin and Zinc during the healing process. It took a further 4 months to clear his system of the antibiotics and steroids and to get him producing his own steroids for probably the first time in his life. He had a fine new layer of skin and a full coat in time for his 5th birthday. Unfortunately, as he had taken in insufficient water when on the dry food diet; his liver and kidneys never fully recovered and he only lived until he was 7 years old.
The responsibility of providing 'optimal food for optimal health' lies with all who decide to include dogs in their lives. Nutrition can be a complicated and exact science but it is not rocket science and as dog carers we have the choice to make ourselves more aware of their needs – unfortunately, our dogs don't.

* * *

Starting Dogs On A Natural Diet

If the puppy has not been fed natural by the breeder then you need to introduce a change of diet gradually – increasing the raw/home cooked gradually – in the meantime here are the home cooked recipes that I use for rescues coming in that I want to change and for getting pups going as weaning commences.

Raw Stuff: (Yes Even The Chicken)

Chicken necks are excellent – very small bones will teach the 'chew' which they all need to learn. Most 'barf' suppliers do necks.

Chicken Wings: Again very good for teaching the chewing technique and good for getting weight on because of the fat content.

Duck: Any part of the duck is good, excellent for putting on weight but pricey if you don't shoot – if you have a local shoot, they usually have some for sale.

Raw/ground minced lamb, chicken or pork: Usually mixed with rice or pasta plus grated carrots or a processed raw veggie mix and some wholemeal mixer.

Fish: Whole heads and all. Oily fish is best, herring, mackerel, sardines, pilchards. Don't worry about the bones – the dog can cope with them but no smoked fish.

Cooked Meals

Meat Porridge

I boil a large chicken or a lamb breast/neck in plain water with some olive/veggie oil added until it is well cooked (as the pup gets older/or the older dog more accustomed, I cook it less and less until it is virtually raw then feed it raw) and falling off the bone. Drain and cool but add to the stock (having first checked there are no bones in it). Add kilo of good quality pasta or rice, throw in the potato/veggie peeling and trimmings from your own dinner (no onion family) and if no veggies that day (you've been to MacDonald's ha-ha) then add either barley, lentils or oats or a combination and cook all out. Pick down the chicken/lamb and combine the lot. Feed in portions with wholemeal mixer added.

Offal – good if you are not meat sensitive
Liver, lites, hearts, tripe, kidney, brains, tongue, etc all good, especially for the next stage feeding as the pup gets older or the older dog adjusts.
Cut into pieces and very lightly boil in plain water with some oats/lentils etc. But feed the veggies raw, either processed down slightly or grated.

I get pig and sheep heads from my butcher which are very cheap, I boil this until cooked then strip everything out and off (many find this too yucky) the skin gets slow roasted until crispy for chews everything except the bone and teeth is cut up put back into the boiling water and used as above.

* * *

Where To Find Your Dog Food

Look for local game butchers and get to know them. Chat, buy some of your meat from them and get them to save anything and everything. You can sort it out once home.

Contact local shoots and see if any of them sell the excess of rabbits etc.

Supermarkets like Lidl, Aldi, Netto, sell human graded cheap meats and cuts and frozen free flow mince at a good price. Get to know their sell-off days, usually Thursday and Monday. They also sell good quality sardines in oil for around 40p a tin.

If you have a local market, get to know the stallholders and go when it's near closing time and buy the bruised fruit and veggies. Our market man now keeps us stuff like bananas and apples and we get them really cheap. If there is a fish man ask him to save things like fish heads and roes and the bruised unsold fish – they would rather sell it for something than dump it.

The larger supermarkets have a huge sell by date turn around. We know that Monday mornings is our Sainsbury's day for the cheap shelf and that Tesco's clear out is on a Friday morning ready for the weekend. Asda have stuff daily. Morrisons not so much but they do sell packs of bones on their fresh meat sectio. Don't forget to also check out the dried goods sell off shelf for dried peas, lentils, rice etc.

Find farm shops that are selling local produce. Try and talk to their suppliers and ask them for the bones, vegetable trimmings etc.

Try and use only human grade foods. These wont have any of the more nasty preservatives in them (like vit K3 for example) that dog food manufactures can use without labeling.

With things like supplements watch out for Holland and Barrets 2 for one offers. Things like oil capsules, honey, sea kelp etc don't need a use by date so stock up.

We only spend on average (excluding the pups of course) 40p per dog per day and we have big dogs with the girls weighing in at 33K and the boys at 40K

Once you up and running it's easy.

* * *

Dietary Requirements For Healthy Dogs

Individual dogs have individual nutritional requirements, even within the same breed, their dietary needs require to be adjusted according to their lifestyle and environment and importantly, for each of the life stages.

There are 6 groups of nutrients:

Proteins
Carbohydrates
Fats
Vitamins
Minerals
Water

Within these groups are the 45 individual nutrients that are needed by dogs in order to stay healthy. The quality of the diet is determined by the appropriate blend of these nutrients not the ingredients that offer them, whilst the ingredients are important as they contribute to the palatability, digestibility and cost, it is the nutritional benefits that affect health.

Protein

Puppies and juveniles require the essential amino acids that are broken down and absorbed during the digestion of proteins in order to grow physically and mature mentally. Due to the accelerated growth at these ages, good quality proteins are needed more than at any other time during a dog's life. A diet that consists of 40% high quality protein is of greater value at this stage than a diet of 70% second-class protein as the conversion of the amino acids produces toxic waste, i.e. nitrogen compounds, which will cause excessive evacuation, thus taking other valuable nutrients with it. By the age of 3 months and up to 1 year of age, a diet consisting of 40% of raw protein will give the adequate protein requirement after biochemical conversion of a 15% intake as long as the quality is still high.

Once the dog is over a year old then the protein requirements need to be assessed according to the individual needs. This will depend on breed, level of activity and exposure to stress. This assessment will require adjusting for lifetime changes, i.e. pregnant and lactating mothers, injury and illness. In adulthood, approximately 5% less protein is required than during juvenility, the important thing to remember is that protein does not produce energy; as the carbohydrates do, and a high protein diet continued over a period of time will produce health problems later in life; with urea and liver functions being overworked in order to rid the body of the nitrogen compounds and other waste.

Obese and older dogs will only require approximately 25% protein in their diet. They require less in order to reduce the strain on the kidneys and liver and only require enough to repair viable damaged tissue. As most forms of protein fed to dogs also have a high fat content, this is the time of life that dogs become obese if overfed protein, one of the most common misconceptions by feeders is that an older dog requires more protein to stay healthy, when in fact the opposite is true.

Fat

Fat is an essential requirement in a dog's diet as it stores and carries the fat soluble vitamins A and E, thus ensuring the omega fatty acids are utilised to maintain coat quality, breeding efficiency and internal organ functions. As it only provides fuel for energy that has to be used immediately; and excess is only extra calories which will lay down fat layers in the body, it is important to control the amounts given in order to avoid obesity in later life.

Puppies and juveniles require no more than 15% of fat in their diets, if too much fat is consumed, then less of the other essential nutrients are taken, resulting in young dogs suffering health problems due to vitamin deficiencies and other nutritional shortages.

Adult and geriatric dogs will only require 10% to 12% of fat content in their diets unless the dog is very active. The energy produced from fat has to be burned off daily and a diet high in fat content will put a strain on the older dogs liver; due to the extra work asked of it in order to convert the excess fatty acids, the heart; due to the fat deposits being laid down in the cardiovascular system and obesity; creating breathing problems and overall poor muscular fitness.

Carbohydrate

Carbohydrates provide the main source of energy by being turned into glucose that the body needs in order to be active. Extra glucose can be stored in the liver and muscles for later use; unlike the energy produced from fat, which has to be burned off daily. The most important forms of carbohydrates are those that are easily digested by the dog. Cellulose, whilst being a good source of energy, is not easy for a dog to digest and care is required in its preparation.

Puppies and juveniles will require 50% to 60% of carbohydrate in their diets, of which 90% should be of easily digestible fibre, otherwise digestive problems will occur.

Adult dogs require approximately 50% of protein unless they are very active working dogs when a minimum of 60 % will be required to produce the extra energy asked for.

Adult dogs require approximately 50% of protein unless they are very active working dogs when a minimum of 60 % will be required to produce the extra energy asked for.

Vitamins and Minerals

It is important to be aware that there is a strong interdependency between minerals; within each other and also with certain vitamins. The most commonly known is that of calcium and vitamin D and calcium and phosphorous. The recommended daily allowance of all minerals and vitamins will be provided in a healthy balanced diet, often any deficiencies are only discovered when there is a problem with health. Calcium and phosphorus maintain the strength of teeth and bone; calcium also helps with the clotting of the blood and helps nerve and muscle function. Phosphorus helps the storage and transfer of energy throughout the body, low doses of both can cause skeletal deformities in growing puppies and juveniles, but high doses of both can also cause serious problems, i.e. excessive bone growth in puppies leading to problems in later life.

Magnesium is required for healthy bones and teeth and for the cardiovascular system and acts as a catalyst for enzyme reaction throughout the body.

Potassium helps the metabolism, nerve and muscle functions and the control of the osmotic balance of body fluids.

Sodium also regulates the body fluids and whilst a deficiency can cause tiredness, fatigue and hair loss, too much will cause a greater amount of water intake and place strain on the kidneys, especially in the older dog.

Iron and copper enhance the efficiency of the blood, cell and enzyme systems, a deficiency of either will produce fatigue and weight loss; even if iron is present in the diet, without copper then anaemia will occur due to the interdependency of these two minerals.

Zinc maintains skin and coat and a deficiency can lead to poor growth rate in puppies, emaciation and in the adult and geriatric dog, testicular atrophy.

Iodine keeps the thyroid gland and thyroid hormones in healthy production, the symptoms for too much are similar to those of too little, tiredness, apathy and poor reproduction.

Selenium acts as an antioxidant and protects the cell membranes but can only work in conjunction with vitamin E. There is a very fine line between a normal and a large dose and is very toxic.

Manganese supports the carbohydrate and fat metabolism by helping the utilisation of produced energy; a deficiency will slow down the rate of growth in young dogs and affect the reproductive systems in adult dogs.

Cobalt is a part of the vitamin B12 molecule and deficiency is unlikely if sufficient B12 is in the diet.

Vitamin A assists vision, keeps skin healthy and helps replace coat loss after moulting. It is toxic in large quantities but deficiencies are rare with a healthy diet.

Vitamin D can be synthesised through the skin when exposed to sunlight and helps the absorption of calcium, deficiency can cause rickets; an illness of the joints and bone, but is quite rare.

Vitamin E protects the cell agonist oxidation and acts with selenium.

Vitamin K regulates the clotting of the blood.

Vitamin B1 (thiamine) works with carbohydrates and a deficiency can lead to severe weight loss due to the carbohydrates not being utilised in the body correctly.

Vitamin B2 is essential for cell growth and repair; a deficiency can lead to skin disorders, eye problems and in older dogs testicular hypoplasia.

Vitamin B6 aids the metabolism of the amino acids; deficiency causes weight loss, anaemia and kidney damage.

Biotin is important for maintaining skin and hair condition and also helps in the metabolism of the amino acids. A deficiency is rare but long-term use of antibiotic and steroidal drugs will cause a serious deficiency with symptoms such as skin ulcers, eczema and pruritus; all of which are often treated with more antibiotics and steroids!

Folic acid is an important catalyst, providing many functions, the most important being the maturation of red blood cells in the bone marrow. Deficiency; unlikely with a healthy diet, produces anaemia with it's associated problems. It is important to ensure that females have an adequate supply during pregnancy or post birth anaemia will occur, especially if there has been blood loss during whelping.

❊ ❊ ❊

Do You Give Your Dogs Fruit And Veg?

Canines are meat eaters, but they do graze and if they're wild canines, then they eat the stomach contents of the grazers that are their prey. My ethos is actually very simple. If they eat it then they 1) like it and 2) they know it's good for them.

Because I feed natural, my dogs from tiny pups onwards, get fruit, vegetables and herb and any rescue dogs that come in very quickly pick up the habit. I am lucky as I have a large garden and we grow stuff, but the one area that always attracts them is the herb garden. One of the things that has always fascinated me is the 'selective' choice on any given day for a 'graze'. I have many examples of this.

Fennel. Amilou was having 'girlie period problems' and I noticed that she would munch the fennel before her blind seasons. Fennel in Egyptian times was a natural contraceptive and 'eased' women problems.

Falkor (now passed away) had pancreatic cancer and would munch away on the new shoots of lemon balm. It helps with liver bile production.

Ami is a watercress freak, she can actually smell it in the fridge if i buy it, but on one of our walks it grows, starting spring all through to late autumn. In winter she will actually break the ice and dig up the shoots. Getting her out of a watercress patch is fun lol. It's a good natural antioxidant and high in folic acid.

They all love the wild garlic shoots that appear in spring and a dog that smells of garlic is less likely to attract ticks and fleas and my males have always liked flowering clover.

There are all sorts of 'myths' about dogs eating grass, for example it makes dogs sick. Well, you know what? They do because it does, grass is a healer! If they are feeling 'off' then the cellulose and fibre and sugars etc, is like us taking liver salts. If they're not sick and just munching then they like the sugars. It's fine, let them do it.

My lot adore fruit and seeds, they will graze the blackberries, sloes, seeds in cow parsley, cherries that are low to ground, windfall apples and plums etc. And because I encourage it and don't do 'leave it', late summer and autumn are a feasting ground for them. In the winter we buy the cheap bruised stuff from the markets and cheap fruit/veggie juice from Aldi etc, to add to their cooked dinner days. Got a dog with a bit of a water infection? Then if the dog is used to fruit juices and you can catch it quick, cranberry juice will work a treat and cheaper than a consult at vets and better than antibiotics.

I am a clicker trainer, one of the rules of clicker training is the high quality of the treat. I had a dog that would do anything for a raw brussel sprout. Cubert when he was a little pup would work fast for peas, I've got all his basic behaviours including the recall at 10 weeks using frozen peas!

My message is don't stop them from choosing to graze, give them raw veg and fruit in their diet and use what they like as a low calories reward when you're training. Let them self heal if they're starting to feel ill before you even know it, they will kick in with what they know they need.

Recipes

How to store these recipes

As a general guide if meat protein is present in recipe then it will last around 3 to 5 days stored in a cool place. If it has second class protein in it eg. cheese, lentils, eggs, etc, then they will store for about 10 days in a cool place. You can use cake tins lined with baking paper – greaseproof. If there is no meat or second class proteins present then it will last around 3 weeks before they go soft like human biscuits.

Pig's Head

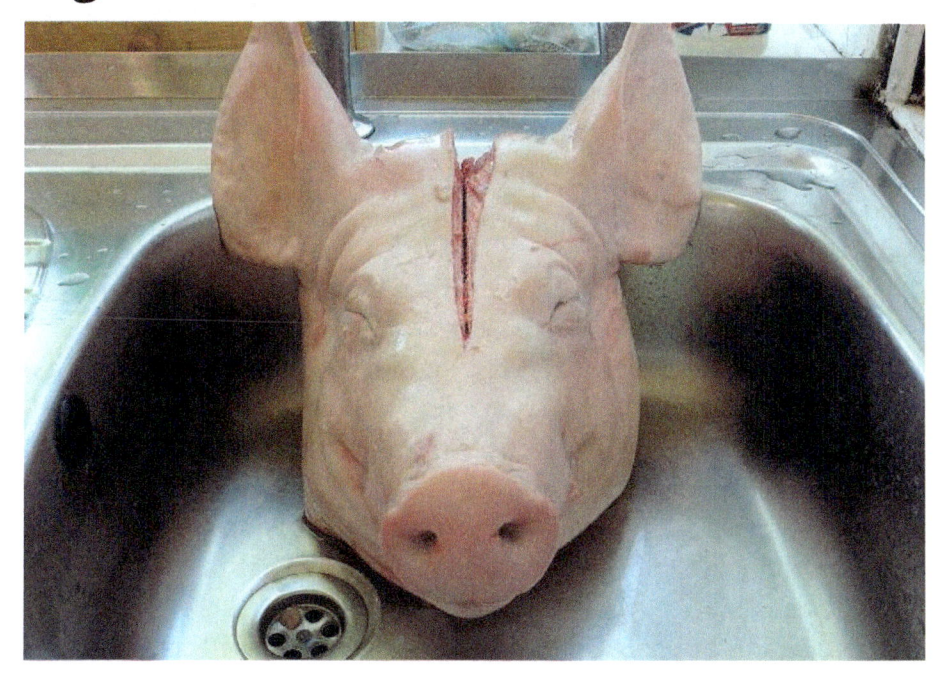

This Is How You Make Real Dog Food

We often get pig heads. Sometimes they come cut in half but often a whole head. If you are not squeamish then they really are an ideal source of dog meat. Let's face it, not so many years ago the components of a pig's head was thought of as good human food. I and my sisters certainly grew up eating it and the dogs got what we couldn't/didn't eat. Brawn, tongue, cheeks, homemade haslet etc.

If you haven't had braised pig cheeks in a thick brown gravy with mash you have missed a real tasty dish and as a teenager coming home drunk(ish), attacking the brawn and spreading it on toast with brown sauce? Wow - 1970's kebab.

Ingredients

1 pig head
Several large potatoes

Some carrots
Bag of rice.

But you can instead chuck in any veg trimmings, barley or couscous you may . No onions.

Method
1. Rinse the pig's head
2. Plunge in large saucepan of boiling water then boil until you can stick a skewer into cheeck area with ease (2 hours +)
3. Lift out of stock. Now this stock will be very fatty. If your dog is healthy and has no eating fat problems like dogs with pancreatitis then add veg trimmings, rice or barley or couscous or pasta to stock and simmer for 15 mins.
4. If your dog cannot do fat, leave to cool, remove solid fat from the top and then use the stock as previous (save that fat, it's brill for roast tatties!)
5. Once head has cooled strip off all the skin. We will come back to the skin in a moment
6. Pick out all the meat. This is cheek area, brain (may have to crack the skull bone), tongue (may have to force the jaws) and pick all the rest of the bones clean.

One average sized pigs head will give you about 20 portions of meat content. We pay £1 for a head and once it's picked down, portion it up and.
Remember this is high quality fat and meat and they don't need the volume as if it came from a tin. A dog about the size of a lab needs no more than 2 to 3 cooked ounces (about 100g) of meat. Add the veggies from the stock and now you have twenty portions of pig head meat and veg/rice/barley/couscous etc. Add 1mug of cheap whole meal mixer to each dinner.
So, 5p for the meat/fat, 5p for the veg, 10p for the rice/barley and 10p for the mixer. That's just 30p to feed a Labrador size dog. Compare that to balls in a bag or tinned meat with 80% water in it!

And the skin?
Next time you have the oven on, place the skin on the baking tray and bake it until crispy. Pork crackling dog treats without the salt and additives.

* * *

Offal

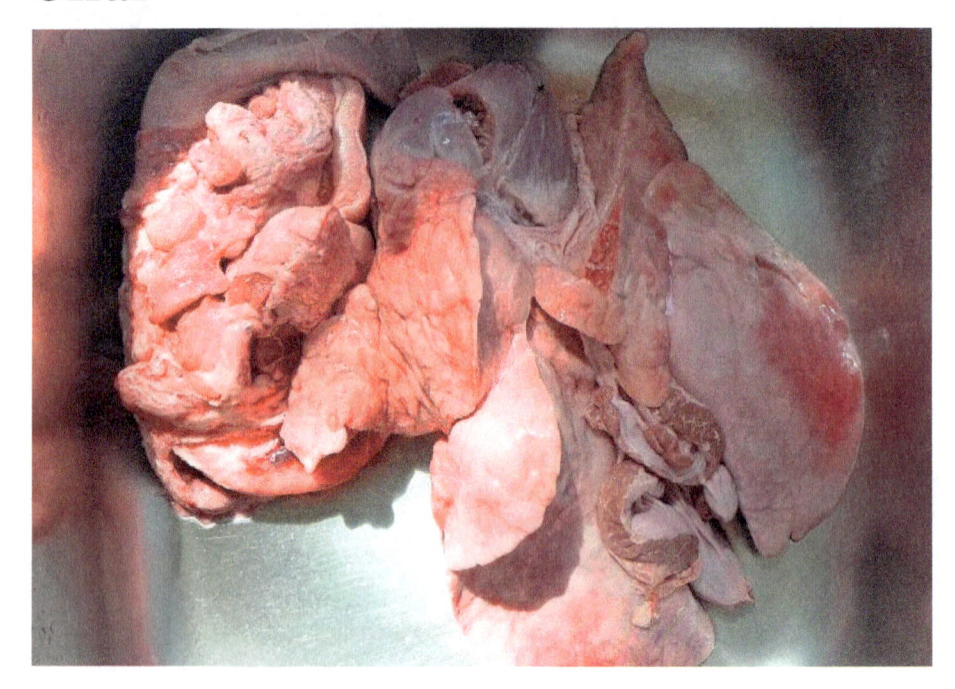

Lites (plucks) are animal lungs and sold as off. They are used in haggis and in faggots and often minced and added to pork for sausages. They are a main food used in tinned dog food, but as tinned dog food is 80% water you are paying a high price for a very cheap source of meat.

If you pay £1 per tin then you are paying 80p for the water and 20p for the meat content and and vegetable scraps added.

As an average they are composed of 75% good quality protein and 25% easily digestible fats. Most game registered butchers will sell you lites very cheaply and because of the high protein content, dogs don't need much of them.

Ingredients

To make dog food using offal, you will need lungs (aka lites/pluck tops) or a lung, heart combo (aka Plucks). Veg trimmings such as potato/carrot/parsnip peelings, the leaves and stalks from cabbage/cauliflower/broccoli etc or a diced up turnip/swede. My dogs love peas and beans and lentils, but any veg that is going a bit limp and sorry for itself is good, but no onions. Add a packet of cheap couscous/pasta, or if your dog isn't rice sensitive then cheap rice.

Method
1. Rinse lites
2. Place in a very large pot and cover with water
3. Bring to the boil and cook for 20/30 minutes
4. Remove lites from pot
5. Add veg trimmings such as potato/carrot/parsnip peelings alongside pasta or rice, to your stock
6. Once veg is cooked, dice the cooked lites and mix with the pasta/rice and veg in pot
7. Allow to cool and divide into portions, freezing what you're not using in the next 2 days

For an average dog of around 20kg the lites, veg and pasta will make 8+ days worth of dinners….add 2/3 mug of plain wholemeal biscuit mixer to the evening meal if you feed twice a day…don't add this in the morning meal.

Ruby loves her homemade dinners

* * *

Liver Cake

This liver cake recipe is very simple to make, cheap and dogs love it. All supermarkets sell liver so it's easy to find but if you can't get liver you can use other ingredients for your cake mix, like minced beef, kidney, heart, chicken livers or even tuna! Once cooked, put what you won't be using in the next couple of days in the freezer until needed. Defrosts in just minutes once out of the freezer. You can top with cream cheese if you want to add frosting. Alternatively, instead of using a cake tin try using a cupcake tray. Liver cake is deal as a treat, a dog birthday cake, selling at fairs etc. We'll be using a 9" cake tin.

Ingredients:

- 500g (1lb) of liver
- 2 Eggs
- 200g (7oz) Wholemeal flour
- 1 crushed garlic clove or 1 small teaspoon of lazy garlic (optional).

• A splash of milk

Method:

1. Add the liver, the eggs, the garlic and a splash of milk to a jug.
2. And blend it. It should look a bit like a smoothie once done.
3. Transfer the mix to a large bowl and add 200g (7oz) of flour.
4. Mix ingredients until it's a thick sticky goo. You can add a bit more flour if it's not thick enough. But it should be fine.
5. Grease a cake tin with a little butter.
6. Empty your mix into cake tin, making sure it's level.
7. Put cake tin into the middle of a preheated oven at 160ºC (320ºF/Gas Mark 3) and cook for about 45 mins.
8. Right, it should now be cooked. Yummy!
9. It's easier to cut while it's still warm.
10. Cut into squares and fridge. Freeze what you won't use in a few days.
11. If your dog is like mine, she will have watched you the entire time.

Flo smells something good!

If you use a cupcake tray, you can make pupcakes. 30 mins cooking time, instead of 45. You can even use cream cheese as frosting.

❊ ❊ ❊

Dehydrated Treats

While researching how to make jerky for dogs I see that there's recipes out there on the web that place raw meat including chicken on the dehydrator while on other websites they tell you to precook the meat first to kill pathogens. A dog becoming sick from such things as Salmonella is rare as their digestive tract is very small so bad bacteria usually gets killed before it can harm the dog. But note that the top temperature of a dehydrator is usually around 70c (160f) which is not enough to kill such pathogens as Salmonella and E. coli. Therefore after drying raw meat I always put it in the oven for 10 minutes at 150ºC to make sure all pathogens are killed.

Oregon state University researched how to make homemade jerky safe and they say that:

"Jerky can be considered "done" and safe to eat only when it has been heated sufficiently to destroy any pathogens present

and is dry enough to be shelf-stable. Shelf-stable means the the jerky can be stored at room temperature and will not support microbial growth."

Oregon state University's method for destroying pathogens:

"Post-drying heating. Placing dried meat strips on a cookie sheet in an oven preheated to 257ºF [126ºC] and heating the strips for 10 minutes effectively eliminates pathogens. This method produces the most traditional jerky."

So after drying any raw meat I place the jerky in the oven for 10 minutes just to be sure. It doesn't change the jerky in any way and gives me peace of mind. Many recipes (mainly for human consumption) use salt or vinegar soak to deal with pathogens in raw meat but both can cause stomach problems in dogs and I want to keep these treats pure and simple.

Before You Start

1. Always wash your hands before you start.
2. Food that has less fat lasts longer as fat can't be dried and will spoil the food faster, so if you're planning to store the treats for long term then trim any fat off the meat before you dry it out.
3. Drying times vary a lot. Temperature, thickness's of food, amount on trays and different machines all affect timing. Your user manual will help and you'll soon get to know when it's done by texture, look and from general experience. The above dehydrator is cheap and perfectly good and what I use but if you want the 'Rolls-Royce' of dehydrators check out Excalibur.
4. Place dehydrated jerky in the freezer (no defrost required) but you can learn more about storing jerky here.
5. Cut meat as thin or as thick as you want but the thicker it is the longer it takes to dry.
6. A very sharp knife for cutting thin slices.
7. You'll be surprised how much food shrinks when dehydrated. Just remember that this is concentrated food and don't give too

much – it's a treat!

Raw Pig Ears

Dried pig ears are expensive to buy but if you can get raw pig ears then they can cost around a third of the price or less. Stick them on the dehydrator and once done you wont be able to tell them apart from the ones you buy in pet shops (except that they may be a lot larger!). They are easy to buy raw online if you have trouble getting them locally.

1. Place raw pig ears on the dehydrator and make sure they are not touching each other.
2. Dry for 16-24 hours. Once dried I place in oven at 257ºF (126ºC) for 10 mins.

Chicken Feet

I first bought dried chicken feet in the pet shop years ago for my new puppy Flo. It's her all time favourite treat. If you ask a local butcher you may able to get raw feet for free else you can buy them raw and by the kilo online. Raw chicken feet take ages to dry so there is no point just drying off a dozen or so. To make the drying time worthwhile I'm gonna be drying off 2 kilos worth of feet which will take around 4-5 days at 70ºC.

1. The first thing to do is give the feet a wee rinse to clean them up.
2. The feet have nails and they are quite sharp so you don't want the dogs eating these when they are dry and brittle so cut them off.
3. Dry for 96 – 120 hours. If your timer only goes up to 48 hours, you'll have to restart the dehydrator a few times. You'll know when they are done when there is no flex in the feet, especially the skin and the padded parts. You want them dry and hard.

Pig Skin

Every super market sells pig skin it for crackling and it's very cheap to buy. Dehydrating pig skin makes a great treat for dogs especially a treat to keep the dog busy – of all the foods here this one will last the longest lasting.

Pig skin dries a little different than pig ears. It's much harder to break down and isn't as brittle as the ear, it's more like rawhide and the dogs just go crazy for it. And like rawhide dogs should be supervised when eating this. When prepping this recipe, cut the pig skin into the sizes you want before you dry as it's too difficult to do it after – it's very, very tough.

1. Slice the skin into strips and lay on dehydrator.
2. Dry at 70ºC for 24 hours.

Tripe

I usw white tripe (dressed) cause it's easier for me to get than green tripe (undressed) – although I do plan to try green tripe in the future. Green tripe is very smelly which is why dogs love it, so be warned when drying it indoors! Every dog owner at one point has bought this treat in the pet shop, now you can have some fun by making tripe jerky at home. Tripe is easy to buy online.

1. Wash tripe and then gently pat dry.
2. Cut into 1 inch strips and place on tray.
3. Dehydrate for around 14 hours at 70ºC (158ºf) followed by a quick 10 minute heat in over.

Beef

If you buy jerky for dogs it's usually either chicken or beef. It's rare to get in this pure high quality form, it's usually very processed and nasty but here we can make a jerky treat worthy of our dogs.

1. Freeze beef for an hour and then slice your lean beef 1/8th of an inch thick.
2. Evenly lay out beef strips on dehydrator tray and make sure no strips are touching each other. Check user instructions for cooking meat. For my dehydrator I'm advised to use the highest temp of 70ºc (158ºf). I will dry this batch for about 7-8 hours. I'll know it's ready if I bend it and it cracks without breaking.

Salmon

Salmon super-food, but a bit oily and wont store as long. But you know what? That oil is super healthy.

1. Freeze for 1 hour to firm salmon. Like the beef slice your salmon into strips about 1/8th of an inch thick.
2. Place salmon on tray while making sure they are evenly spread and not touching. Check user guide for drying instructions. These will be dried at 70ºC (158ºf) for 8-10 hours or until they are hard and dry all the way through followed by 10 minute stint in the oven.

Liver

A great alternative to dried liver treats cooked in the oven. Hardly any smell and very clean to handle. You'll want to cut thin strips of liver to reduce dehydrating time.

1. Wash, pat dry and slice into thin strips.
2. Space evenly on tray. Dry for around 10-12 hours followed by a 10 minute stint in the oven!

Sea Bass Jerky

I found two boneless fillets of Sea Bass going very cheap in the local market. Because of it's low fat content Sea Bass is ideal for drying, packed with flavour with a strong fishy aroma. Yummy and a real winner with dogs. I couldn't stop eating the stuff. Yummy!

1. Put in freezer for an hour to firm fish then slice into strips.
2. Place strips on tray and dehydrate. Will take around 9 hours to dry then put them in the oven for 10 mins.

Chicken

Chicken breast is very easy to buy and many pet treat manufactures sell it dried, but it's very expensive. Trim off any bits of fat.

1. Wash hands, wash chicken, pat dry and cut thin strips.
2. Place chicken strips evenly and without touching on dehydrator tray. After around 8-10 hours they are dry.
3. Place in the oven for 10 minutes at 150ºC (300ºf) to make sure it's completely safe and free from any bacteria.
4. Place in freezer for when you need them. No defrost required.

Rabbit

I bought a rabbit from the butchers but because it's just so boney I'll boil it first, take all the meat off the bone and then dry it.

1. Place rabbit in a pot, bring to boil and simmer for 2 hours.
2. Once cooled take all the meat of the bone.
3. Place on the dehydrator at 70c for 6-8 hours and it's done!

Heart

Heart is ideal for turning into jerky because it's just pure muscle and apart from a little bit of fat on the outside it's very lean. Because it is so lean and dense make sure that strips are cut thinly to reduce dehydrating time.

1. Wash the heart, it may contain clotted blood.
2. Trim off any fat, pat dry and slice into thin strips.
3. Place on dehydrator and dry for around 12 hours. (Time varies on thickness of strips) followed by 10 mins in the oven.

Kidney Crisps

Using Ox kidney you can make great crisps with a real crunch. Cheap to buy and they smell like bacon – dogs love them! In Ox kidney there is a large bit of fat in the middle, cut that out if you plan to store.

1. Freeze the kidney first and then cut into very thin slices.
2. Place 'crisps' on tray. Dehydrate for 12 hours at 70c and then

heat in oven for 10 mins afterwards.

Pig Snout

Just for fun I bought a pig snout when ordering a delivery of fresh meat for the dogs. Very high value, the dogs go crazy for it. Lots of yummy meat. Huge success but drying pig snouts aren't practical as they are not easy to get but fun and totally delicious.

1. Place whole pig snout on the dehydrator. Dry for 24 hours at 70ºC. It's just pure delicious meat!

Non Meat Ideas

Dehydrators are also excellent for drying fruit and vegetables so things like bananas, apples and sweet potatoes can be dried to make dog treats. For me I prefer to use meat simply because my dog prefers it.

Sia can smell the meat drying

✻ ✻ ✻

Sardine Oatcakes

The Original Recipe

This is personally my favourite. If you are in need of super high-value treats – you just found them! Your dog will love these oatcakes, they are tasty, healthy, smell great, and just so easy to make! And from preparation to cooking time they take less than one hour!

The dough is more like paper mache than biscuit dough. So alternatively you can use a silicone mould instead of a biscuit cutter.

For a more traditional looking oatcake replace 1 quarter of your rolled oats with pinhead oatmeal – but not necessary.

Ingredients

• 2 tins of sardines in oil (2x120g)
• 1 crushed garlic clove (or 1 small teaspoon of crushed garlic. No powder)
• 60g (1/3 cup) of wholemeal flour

• 300g (1 1/3 cups) of oats
• 150ml Chicken broth (homemade is best)
• 1 egg

Method

1. Make around 150ml (1/4 pint) of stock. Chicken will do. If using cubes get the low salt ones.
2. Add the two tins of sardines to a bowl (including the oil)!
3. Mash the sardines thoroughly with a fork!
4. Add 1 crushed garlic clove or 1 teaspoon of chopped garlic
5. Add one egg
6. Add the 300g (10oz) of oats and 60g (2oz) of wholemeal flour
7. Add a little of broth to bowl. To start with try adding 1/3 of your broth.
8. Mix ingredients with your hands and make a dough ball! Too dry? Add more broth. Too wet? Add some flour or oatmeal.
9. Roll out and cut out biscuits!
10. Place dog biscuits on baking tray and place into a preheated oven at 190°C (370°F) for around 20-25 mins.

If you've made these before, you will know what to expect!

✳ ✳ ✳

Bone Broth

Bone broth is a immune boosting super food and ideal for getting sick pets back on their feet and for maintaining the health of an active dog. Even sick dogs that are not eating will enjoy a bowl of broth and you can add it to their food to help them eat.

Bone broth for dogs is great as it's packed with minerals like like calcium, phosphorus, magnesium and potassium in forms that are easily absorbed by your dog . Rich in amino acids like glycine and proline they help maintain a healthy digestion and keeping your dog calm. The collagen in the bones protects and heals the mucosal lining of the digestive tract aiding in the digestion of nutrients and the gelatin supports fur, skin and nail growth while helping joint pain and inflammation. Marrow helps provide the body with materials needed for healthy blood cells and immune development. **It's perfect for flu season for dogs and people.**

Apple Cider Vinegar

You need apple cider vinegar to help break the bones down and leach all the goodness out. Apple cider vinegar is also great for deterring parasites, is antibacterial and antifungal, improves and conditions the coat, relieves arthritis and improves digestion.

Organic Bones

You can use chicken, pork or beef bones but if possible get organic bones and with beef bones try to get grass fed. Grass fed is higher in Omega 3's. It's also higher in conjugated linoleic acid (CLA) which is anti-inflammatory and anti-carcinogenic. Grass fed is also higher in vitamin E, vitamin A, glutathione and antioxidants. Pigs raised outdoors have a better Omega 3/Omega 6 ratio and more mono-unsaturated fat which is more resistant to high heat.

Cooking Methods

You can really improve the health of your dog by learning how to make dog food that's delicious, simple and healthy and bone broth is as easy as it gets. You'll know when the broth is ready when the bones start to soften and get crumbly/chalky. In a pressure cooker it takes about 4 hours but you can also do it in a pot or slow cooker which will require between 8-24 hours of simmering. Once cooked discard the bones, it's just the broth you want. Dogs should never be fed cooked bones.

Shelf Life

Broth just lasts a few days even in the fridge regardless if it's for humans or dogs... the general rule is freeze it until it's needed.

Ingredients

· 1kg of bones
· 1 cup of apple cider vinegar
· 1-2 cloves of garlic (optional)

Method

1. Add your marrow bones to your pot or pressure cooker

2. Add 1 cup of apple cider vinegar to pot

3. Then fill pot with water to just cover the bones

4. If using a pressure cooking, cook for 4 hours. If using the stove or slow cooker then simmer between 8-24 hours - topping up with water when needed.

Flo, you're such a good girl, yes you are!

❀ ❀ ❀

Dried Liver

The Definitive Training Teat

This dog treat can't be beat. This is what I use for treats when I'm walking all my dogs, and if you do this you will see why they're the best dog training treats you can get!

It's very cheap to buy liver from your local supermarket or butcher (much cheaper than branded treats and a whole lot better for your dog).

hey are ideal for training and to get the attention of your dog and get control back when you are outside.

Cleaning the oven tray can be a pain after drying liver so cover with tin foil or use disposable foil trays. Dried liver is gorgeous and has a nice smell, I even like eating it but it can make your clothes smell if you carry it in them so use a treat bag when out and about.

Ingredients

A packet of liver (any liver will do).

Method
1. Get yourself some liver. Any liver will do
2. Rinse the blood of the liver
3. Wrap a baking tray in kitchen foil
4. Lay your liver on the tray. Preheat your oven to 120c (250f/Gas mark 1). Cook for 1½ - 2 hrs or until fully dry
5. Cut into little squares and fridge what you will use in a few days and freeze the rest

Flo you are getting some, don't worry!

❊ ❊ ❊

Liver Dog Biscuit

The Mother Of All Dog Biscuits?

Bev is our in-house canine behaviourist/dietitian and years ago I decided to try and make her favourite dog biscuit recipe and they turned out so well! Every dog I walked last week loved them far more than I could've ever have hoped for. Even the dogs that aren't food orientated stopped and took notice! I had strangers dogs coming up to me and then try to tear them out of my pocket and some people asking me to make some for them while others insisted I should be selling them!

For this recipe you'll need…

Ingredients

- 1lb/450g pigs liver
- 1lb/2 cups of cornflour
- 170g / 3/4 cup potato flour or semolina
- 1 egg plus milk if more liquid needed
- 2 grated carrots or a grated apple

· 1 clove of fresh garlic (optional)

Method

1. Cut 450grams of liver into chunks and then blend
2. Add half a cup of grated apple to blended liver, or add half a cup of grated carrot instead
3. Add one grated clove of garlic (optional)
4. Add 450g/2 cups of cornflour
5. Add ¾ cups / 170g potato flour or semolina
6. Add an egg, a splash of milk and mix thoroughly
7. Roll out, cut and bake at 350 F/180 C for 15-20 mins

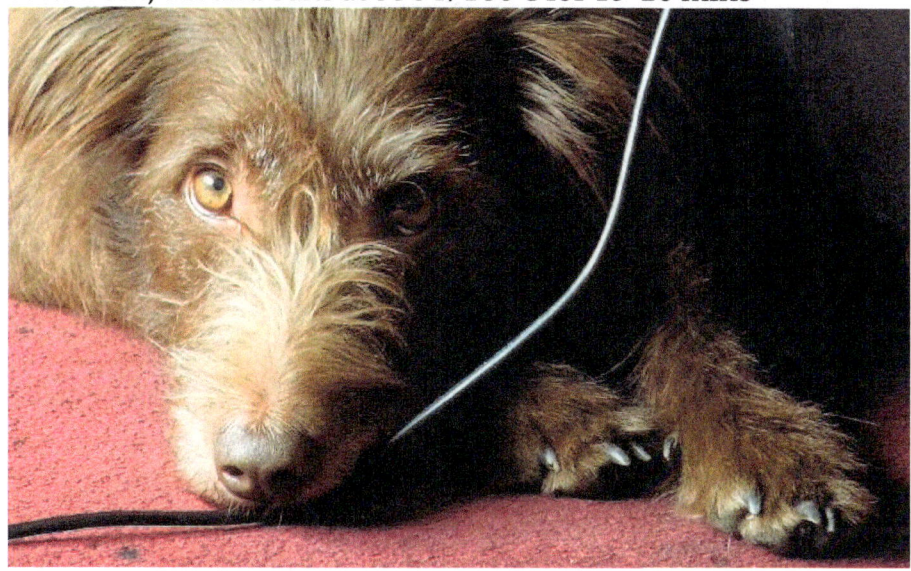

Ruby knows I'm making something... extra special!

❋ ❋ ❋

Kong Stuffing Recipes

The Art Of Kong Stuffing

It's not difficult to learn, but there are requirements for them to work, both for the dog and the human to be satisfied. First you need to decide what the kong is for. Is it a meal in itself? A reward for being good? A treat to be left with when you go out between meals? Whatever it's function there are some rules to follow:

1. The filling has to be at the correct consistency. If it is too hard to get out dog will become frustrated and bored with it. If it is too soft then it will go too fast and the dog will be left feeling unsatisfied and bored ...these apply especially if given one to amuse while you are out and the object was to keep dog occupied to prevent destruction etc.

2. It has to be the correct kong, as in the correct size for the dog's mouth and tongue and of the right hardness and density. You do not want the dog to eat the kong...you will end up with a huge vet bill.

3. Until the dog understands the concept of eating from a kong, never leave alone and unsupervised and if your dog has guarding

tendencies then you need to work on the 'mine' 'yours' training with it...a kong, like a bone is a high resource.

4. A kong is not a toy: you wouldn't allow your dog to play with his/her food dish...don't allow the dog to play with a kong. It is yours not the dog's and is given at your say so and as such a powerful training and bonding aid.

5. It has to taste good...be appealing to the dog and have healthy ingredients; the less commercial junk in the better. Below are tasty and delicious dog food ideas to fill your dog's Kong.

Stuffing Consistency

The stuffing needs to be firm but not hard...about the consistency of pate of soft cheese to begin with. It is easier to make them up while the filling is still warm or at least at room temperature; you can then leave them in the fridge overnight to firm up to the consistency of firm chilled pate. As the dog works at the filling it will soften with the warmth of his/her paws and the action of the saliva. Frozen kongs (we call them doggy lollies in this house) are good as a treat on hot days and help add more fluids into the system. My dogs love frozen fruity kongs on a hot day...but you might want to give those outside.

Size And Type

Check the information on the packet...manufacturers give indications of 'toughness' but you know the power of your own dogs jaw...if your dog can destroy hard substances then you will need the heavy black kong. If you have a puppy you are kong training then the soft light blue one will be best. If it is in substitute of a meal then it will need to be large enough to take the equivalent of what would normally go in a dish.

Banana And Honey

1. Cut of the end of a ripe banana (2 if using the large kong) and block the small hole at the bottom of the kong. Slice 3 or 4 thin pieces and put to one side.

2. Mash the remaining banana in a bowl

3. Add a tablespoon of olive oil to bowl
4. Add a tablespoon of honey and mix
5. Fill kong with banana mash
6. Place the sliced pieces on the top sealing the large end. Smear with a little oil and put in fridge to set for an hour.

Cream Cheese And Apple
1. Dice an apple into very small bits
2. Mix with cream cheese until soft enough to pack into kong
3. Mix with cream cheese until soft enough to pack into kong

Peanut Butter And Meat Paste
1. Seal the small hole of the Kong with peanut butter then smear peanut butter all around the insides
2. Create layers of the butter and meat paste until it is full, ending with a peanut butter layer
3. Refrigerate until firm

Savoury Variety
1. After sealing the small end using peanut butter, cream cheese or butter, stand the kong in an egg carton
2. Fill with a little cooked rice, couscous or cooked lentils or barley
3. Fill with bone broth and freeze for 24 hours

Dairy Variety
1. After sealing the small end using peanut butter, cream cheese or butter, stand the kong in an egg carton
2. Fill the kong 3/4 full with goats milk
3. Fill the remainder of the kong with plain yoghurt… you can also add some pureed fruit and/or honey to the yoghurt if you wish. Freeze for 24 hours

Quick Kong Recipe Ideas
Mash a tin of sardines in oil into the Kong for an instant delicious ready to eat Kong. Freeze to make it last even longer.
Fill a Kong with Brussels Pâté and give straight to dog or put in

freezer to keep the dog busy for longer.

Ruby loves her Kong!

Gluten Free Biscuits

Treats For Sensitive Dogs

My canine dietitian gave me a new biscuit recipe to try. When I made this recipe the first time I took ALL the biscuits with me while I did my dog walking and the dogs just loved them. By the end of the day, I had none left! Thumbs up from the dogs!

This gluten free dog treat recipe is easy to make and can be done within an hour, with little mes. The great thing is you can add your dog's favourite food to flavour it! Just note that potato flour can be quite hard to source from your local supermarket but most health shops sell it and it's easy to buy online.

Ingredients

- 2 mugs of potato flour (240g)
- 2 tablespoons of olive oil
- 1 tablespoon of honey
- Water to mix

We're using apple and cheese to flavour but you can use whatever your dog likes e.g. chopped liver, ground beef, fruit etc.

Method
1. Add 2 mugs of potato flour into a bowl
2. Add 2 tablespoons of olive oil and 1 tablespoon of honey
3. Mix into a crumble like mixture
4. Add a handful of grated cheese
5. And a grated apple (no seeds)
6. Add a little water and make a dough
7. Roll out like a thin sausage and slice
8. Place on baking tray and put in oven at 180°C. Cooking times vary for ingredients and size of biscuits but these biscuits will cook for 30 mins

Brodie loves them!

❊ ❊ ❊

Gingerbread Men

A Homemade Travel Sickness Remedy For Dogs

Add ginger to biscuits and you can make a delicious dog treat. Ginger has been known for a long time to be very effective in combating motion sickness in dogs as well as people. These biscuits are easy to make and dogs think they are very tasty whether they're traveling or not!

Ingredients
170g (6oz) self-raising flour
85g (3oz)peanut butter
60ml (4 tablespoons)hot water
10 grams (2 teaspoons)ground ginger
2 grams (1/2 teaspoon) cinnamon

Method
1. Add the peanut butter to a bowl
2. Add the hot water

3. Give it a good mix

4. Now add the flour, the cinnamon and ginger

5. Now add a little water, just enough to make a dough, roll up your sleeves and really mix

6. Roll out to 1/4 inch thick and preheat oven to 200°c (390°f)

7. Cut out biscuits and place on baking tray

8. Cook for 15-20 mins until golden brown

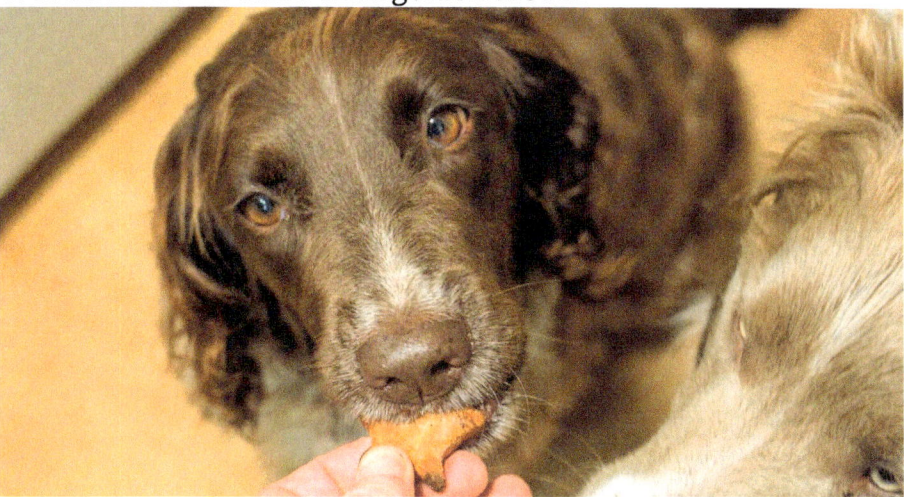

Give to dog. Very tasty!

Puppy Rusks

These puppy teething rusks are large and thick for a reason so if you break them up into small treats then you're missing the point. The point being that they're large so the pup can spend some time biting into this rather than your furniture. Right, let's get this puppy biscuit recipe started!

Ingredients
Packet of thyme and parsley stuffing mix, cheap supermarket packet.
2 mugs of oats
1 mug flour
1 beaten egg
Hot water to mix

Method
1. Add a packet of thyme and parsley stuffing mix to a large bowl
2. Add 2 mugs of oats to bowl

3. Add a mug of flour
4. Add a beaten egg
5. Now add some hot water, create a dough ball and leave to rest
6. Roll out to 1/2 inch thick and cut out biscuits with large cutter
7. Bake at 140° C or gas mark 3 for 50-60 mins or until rock hard

Leave to cool and give to teething pup, or as a reward to a good dog

❈ ❈ ❈

Teeth Soothing Biscuits

For Teething Pups Or Oldies With Worn Teeth

Ginger is good for sore teeth and gums and chamomile is a calmer and reduces anxiety. Chamomile tea is made by steeping dried chamomile in hot water and straining but you can buy chamomile tea bags.

A slice of ginger root rubbed on gums will bring immediate relief for sore gums.

These biscuits that are crunchy on the outside but softer in the middle are good for teething puppies or oldies who may have worn teeth and sore gums with the added benefit of sweet-smelling breath.

This can be made in a food processor, but it's easy to do by hand. I'm also using a large biscuit cutter but use any size you like. They should be quite large though.

Ingredients
250 gm (9oz) of rolled oats

250 gm (9oz) of wholemeal flour
250 gm (9oz) of smooth peanut butter
4 teaspoons of baking powder
2 teaspoons tumeric (Buy Here)
50 gm (2oz) grated fresh ginger or 3 teaspoons ground
Chamomile tea (or chicken stock or water) to mix
We're using this biscuit cutter

Method

1. Make a fresh cup of Chamomile tea and let it infuse and cool (or use chicken stock instead)
2. Add 250 gm (9oz) of oats to a large bowl
3. Add 250 gm (9oz) of wholemeal flour
4. Add 250 gm (9oz) of smooth peanut butter to mix bowl
5. Add 2 teaspoons of turmeric
6. Add 4 teaspoons of baking powder
7. Add 50 gm (2oz) grated fresh ginger or 3 teaspoons ground
8. Give it all a good mix
9. Slowly add enough Chamomile (or chicken stock) to make a pastry
10. Get your hands in and knead
11. Leave to rest for 30 minutes in the fridge
12. Roll out to about 2cm thickness (just less than 1 inch), cut into shapes and place on baking tray
13. Place tray in a preheated oven at 200c (gas mark 7) for 40 mins
14. 40 minutes later and they are done. They need to be crunchy on the outside but softer in middle

If dog is sitting nice…

Jelly Babies

Are These The Healthiest Dog Treats In The World?

For this recipe all you need is gelatin, bone broth, a little garlic paste and a mould to set it in – how could it be any easier than that? Not just super tasty but super healthy too. Gelatin is great for the skin, nails, coat and joints. Bone broth is anti inflammatory, great for the blood, the immune system and aids digestion. Garlic keep fleas, ticks and worms away, cleans the blood and is anti fungal, anti-bacterial and antiviral.

No sugar, no gluten, no preservatives, just pure goodness in a tasty treat that your dog will love. Just 3 ingredients needed to make this simple dog treat recipe that makes your dog even healthier.

Ingredients

2 ½ tablespoons of gelatin
140ml (1/2 cup) of bone broth
¼ teaspoon of garlic paste

Method

1. Pour the bone broth into a small pot
2. Add the garlic & gelatin
3. Heat gently on a low heat for about 10 minutes, until all the gelatin has dissolved. Stir regularly
4. Once it's all dissolved, pour into a jug and then pour into a silicon mould before it cools

Duffy's had one, but now she wants more!

❋ ❋ ❋

Low Fat Dog Biscuits

Ideal For Dogs Suffering From Pancreatitis Or On A Diet

A pancreatic diet is first and foremost very low fat but also with no added processed sugars, so as an example in this recipe the only fat is what is in banana and the only sugars are the natural simple ones already in the ingredients, hence no butter, no oil, no honey, no malt and no fats.

Inflammation of the pancreas is generally referred to as pancreatitis. It is very painful for dogs and humans. The pancreas is the organ that produces enzymes that assist with the processing of sugars in the body.

Feeding a dog that has been diagnosed with this is condition can be a bit mind-blowing, but all is not lost and it doesn't mean you cannot feed natural or give treats. I like homemade as I know 100% what's in them.

It is scary, frightening even, when you see that huge pool of blood filled diarrhea and your heart sinks into your gut and your shaking from head to toe then yep, all sorts goes through the brain.

Please, do not self diagnose this possible condition, if you not sure and there is poo looking like unset blackcurrant jam or jelly, then vets asap.

For this recipe we are using Pinhead oats, but you can use rolled oats found everywhere. Pinhead oats can be bought on Amazon.

Ingredients

1 medium ripe banana
2 large carrots
28ml/2 fl oz apple or cranberry or vegetable juice (no citrus juice) mixed with equal amount of water.
340g/12 oz of polenta (or wholemeal flour or semolina)
226g/8oz of rolled oats (I'm using pinhead oatmeal)

Method

1. Add a medium sized banana to a large bowl
and mash it
2. Grate two carrot into the bowl
3. Add 226g (8oz) of rolled oats or pinhead oats and add to your bowl
4. Add 340g (12oz) of polenta (you can use wholemeal flour or semolina instead) to your bowl
5. Add 56ml (2 fl oz) of apple juice to measuring jug (or use cranberry or vegetable juice (but no citrus juice) and add the same amount again of water
7. Add your liquid to the mixing bowl then give the ingredients a good mix
8. Now is the time to add more liquid if needed. This is dependant on your ingredients. Knead thoroughly. Really work it with your hands. You want it to be just like a pastry or scone mix
9. Roll out your dough to around 1/4 inch thick and cut into shapes
10. Place in oven at 200c (392F/Gas mark 6)

11. Cook for around 20-30 mins depending on thickness

My dogs are trying to tell me something, but I don't know what!

Tuna Loaf

Make In Just 10 Minutes

This tuna loaf dog treat recipe was given to me by Alison, the owner of Brodie and Harris! It's one of the simplest treat recipes you will ever make and done within 10 minutes! We're gonna be using a 1.1L food storage container found in any supermarket to make this but you can use a large bowl and cover with a large plate.

Ingredients

2 tins of tuna in oil or water
2 eggs
160g of flour (wholemeal or plain)
1 garlic clove or 1 small teaspoon of lazy garlic

Method

1. Add 2 tins of tuna in oil (use the oil/water) to a bowl
2. Add two eggs
3. Add 160g (5½ oz) of flour
4. Add 1 crushed garlic clove or 1 small teaspoon of chopped garlic

5. Mix everything together to form a thick paste-like consistency.

6. Spread into a microwave-safe container or bowl with a plate on top

7. Lay lid slightly ajar if using a container and cook for 4 minutes, rest for 1, then cook for another minute

8. It's very hot once cooked, so tap out of container and leave to cool

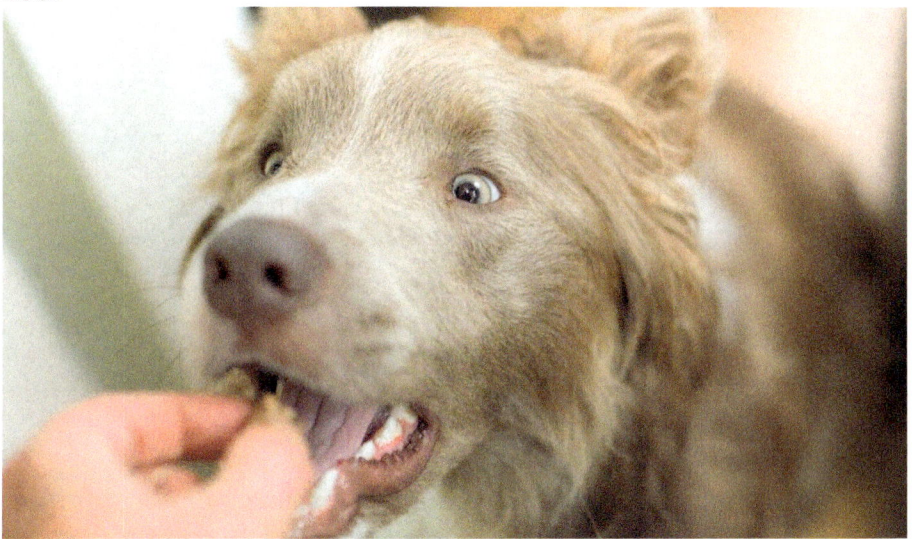

Have a taste test with the dog. Fridge what you will use in a few days and freeze the rest.

❁ ❁ ❁

Calming Biscuits

A Diabetic-Friendly, Calming Dog Treat Recipe

These cinnamon biscuits are good for periods of anxiety; vet visits, times of separation, groomers, stressful situations, etc.

Cinnamon is a strong antioxidant and anti-inflammatory and also lowers blood sugar.

As the sweetness comes from the sweet potatoes and bananas, this is an ideal treat for dogs with diabetes.

Sweet potato is a natural soporific so is a good relaxant and an excellent natural sleep aid. They are also a good source of vitamins and minerals.

Ingredients

A large mixing bowl
1 sweet potato (around 250-300 gm)
1 medium soft banana
170 gm (6oz) rolled or nibbed oats
115 gm (4oz) wholemeal flour
1 egg

3 teaspoons of cinnamon

Method

1. Peel and dice your sweet potato
2. Boil sweet potatoes until soft and then drain
3. Mash. Leave in the warm pan without lid, to allow the excess water to steam away
4. When potatoes are cool, transfer to a mixing bowl
5. Add a banana and mash
6. Add 170 gm (6oz) rolled or nibbed oats
7. Add 3 teaspoons of cinnamon
8. Add an egg
9. Combine the ingredients. The consistency needs to be soft enough to handle but not wet. More oats can be added to firm
10. Using a soup or pudding spoon as a measure, form into balls (damp hands will stop them sticking)
11. Place on a lightly greased baking sheet or tray
12. When they are all on tray use a fork to squash down
13. Bake in a preheated for 30 to 35 minutes (200C/400F/Gas Mark 6)
14. Once cooked, take out the oven and leave to cool

Expect nosey dogs to appear

* * *

Flapjacks

Low Fat, Healthy Dog Treat Recipe

Lentils are an excellent source of iron, fibre and second class protein. Being low in calories but high in fibre helps dogs that seem hungry all the time to feel more full. Great for dogs on a diet or having a history of not self-emptying full anal glands. Once a manual gland emptying starts then you got it for life without dietary changes .

Whilst they are a great supplements for diabetic pets; as they help prevent blood sugar spiking, they should only be given in small quantities to dogs that have a diagnosed history of heart problems. They do not cause but can affect so If anyone needs guidance regarding either conditions and diet please comment below.

Ingredients

1 tablespoon olive oil
110g (4 oz) grated cheese

1 tin of carrots (rinsed out)
200g (7oz) split red lentils rinsed and drained
110g (4 oz) rolled oats
1 tablespoon of lemon juice
2 tablespoons of honey
1½ pints of chicken stock

Method

1. Make 1½ pints of chicken stock
2. Put 200g (7oz) of rinsed red lentils in a pan and cover with just enough stock, keeping back any extra .
3. Add 1 tbsp of olive oil and 1 tbsp of lemon juice
4. Bring to the boil and cook for 20 minutes until lentils are well cooked and soft
5. Strain lentils reserving any stock adding it to stock left in jug
6. Place the drained lentils in a bowl. Now add the wash rinsed tinned carrots
7. Whilst still warm mash down or pulse the carrots and lentils
8. Add a teaspoon of Tumeric
9. Add 110g (4oz) of grated cheese to bowl
10. Stir the ingredients through. The mixture needs to be firm but with all oats well mixed in. Add more stock if required
11. Add 110g (4oz) of rolled oats to bowl
12. Add 2 tbsp of honey and give it all a good mix
13. Grease your baking tray
14. Roll onto balls and lay on tray. No bigger than a golf ball.
15. **Important:** Place in middle shelf of a preheated oven at 160c (Gas Mark 3) then start checking after 30 mins but can take up to 50 mins to cook as they are cooking slowly
16. Once they begin to brown they are pretty much done. They will be soft and fragile when they are hot after taking them out of oven but really firm up as they cool.

I now have Flo's attention

✳ ✳ ✳

Beet Bites

Beetroot is a good source of vitamin C, fibre, folate, manganese, and potassium, and sold everywhere. This biscuit recipe makes a nice hard crunchy dog treat using precooked beetroot I bought on sale in my local Co-op. Add some oats, flour, a beaten egg, and just for fun some golden breadcrumbs and you have a purplish, tasty dog treat.

Ingredients
3 cooked beetroots
2 Eggs
280g (10z) rolled oats
140g (5oz) plain flour
60g (2oz) golden breadcrumbs
100ml (4 fl oz) of meat stock (low salt if using cubes)

Method
1. Add 60g (2oz) of breadcrumbs to a mixing bowl

2. And 280g (10oz) of rolled oats and 140g (5oz) of plain flour

3. Add a beaten egg

4. Blend 3 precooked beetroots and add to bowl

5. Give it a good mix

6. Add just a little at a time, add enough stock to turn ingredients into a pastry. 100ml should be more than enough

7. Roll into a ball and leave for 10 minutes

8. Roll to a half-inch thick and cut out shapes

9. Place on a baking tray and cook at 150c (Gas mark 2) for around 1hr 30 mins or until rock hard

Give treat to one lucky dog

❀ ❀ ❀

Birthday Cake

An Easy Carrot Cake Recipe And Ideal For Birthday Cakes

Just for a bit of fun and I know there's quite a few people that like baking birthday cakes for their dogs. Nothing fancy in this recipe, just a simple carrot cake using a few local ingredients found anywhere and easy to make. Dogs love it and for the icing, we are using cream cheese which dogs also love. Perfect for a good dog or a special occasion.

For this recipe we're gonna be using a 9" cake tin.

Ingredients

170g (6oz) of self-raising flour
170g (6oz) of wholemeal flour
2 tsp of cinnamon
2 tsp of baking powder
4 eggs

A splash of milk
1 tub of cream cheese

Method

1. Add 170g (6oz) of wholemeal flour to a bowl
2. Add 170g (6oz) of self-raising flour
3. Add 2 tsp of baking powder
4. Add 2 tsp of cinnamon powder
5. Give it all a mix
6. Grate 340g (12oz) of carrots and add to bowl
7. Add 4 eggs
8. Add a decent splash of milk
9. And give it a right good mix
10. Grease a cake tin with butter and add your mix
11. Add cake tin to a preheated oven set at 170c (Gas mark 3) and cook for 35-40 mins
12. Once cooked leave to cool in the cake tin
13. Now add the cream cheese to the top, as your frosting

It's Flo's birthday!

✱ ✱ ✱

Thank You
For Buying This Book

Dedicated to Ruby
2007 - 2020

Books By This Author

How To Be A Dog Walker - A Pocket Guide

A pocket guide on how to start a dog walking business. Written by a real dog walker with over 12 years of experience. Learn the basics and get ready to start with confidence. The most popular guide on starting a dog walking business ever written in the UK!

- Learn what is involved
- Learn how to market your business online and offline
- Learn what you need to get started
- Tips on how to manage dogs in groups
- FREE First Aid Guide included
- Free Contract/Form Templates
- Advice on taxes and insurance
- And lots more!

Printed in Dunstable, United Kingdom